Sports Stars

MAGIC JOHNSON

Court Magician

By Richard Levin

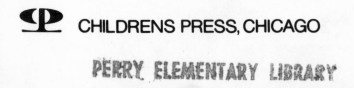 CHILDRENS PRESS, CHICAGO

Cover photograph: Bob Kingsbury
Inside photographs courtesy of the following: Bill Jennaro, pages 6, 29, 36, 39, 44;
Goerge Fox, pages 8 (bottom), 11, 12, 14, 17, 18; Don Grayston, pages 8 (top), 20, 21, 22
Kevin W. Reece, pages 26, 35; Howard Zryb, page 28; and Ira W. Golden, page 41

Library of Congress Cataloging in Publication Data

Levin, Rich, 1943-
  Magic Johnson, court magician.

  (Sports stars)
  SUMMARY: A brief biography of an outstanding
basketball player who was instrumental in the Los
Angeles Lakers' successful bid for the 1979-80 NBA title.
    1. Johnson, Earvin, 1959—Juvenile literature.
2. Basketball players—United States—Biography—
Juvenile literature. [1. Johnson, Earvin, 1959-
2. Basketball players. 3. Afro-Americans—Biography]
I. Title. II. Series.
GV884.J63L48   796.32'3'0924 [B] [92] 80-25814
ISBN 0-516-04313-7

Sports Stars

MAGIC JOHNSON

Court Magician

Earvin "Magic" Johnson, Jr. was only 21 years old. He already was one of the best basketball players in the world.

He is known as Magic. People think he does magic on the basketball court.

His impossible plays look easy. He plays the guard position. He is six feet eight. He is much taller than most of the players who play guard. Most guards are about six feet to six four or six five. His height gives him a big edge.

He also plays with great joy. He cheers on his teammates. When one makes a good play, he slaps their palms. The fans love this.

But above all, Magic is a winner.

In four years he led his teams to championships on three different levels.

In 1977 the Vikings of
Everett High won the Michigan
State Championship (below),
and two years later Michigan State
won the NCAA. Magic
played on both teams.

In 1977 his Everett High School team won the Michigan state championship. Two years later Magic was in second year college at Michigan State. The Spartans won the National Collegiate Athletic Association (NCAA) title. Magic's rookie professional season was 1979-80. His team, the Los Angeles Lakers, won the National Basketball Association (NBA) title.

"I do whatever it takes to win," Magic says. "I could score a lot more points if I wanted to. But that is not the object of the game. The object is to win. And I try to make sure my teams do that."

Magic grew up in Lansing, Michigan. He was known as Earvin or E. J. (his initials). He got his nickname from a sportswriter. The sportswriter's name was Fred Stabley, Jr. He covered Everett High games for *The Lansing State Journal.*

Stabley tells how he gave Magic the name.

"The first game Everett played that year, they got by Holt by one point," he says. "And Holt wasn't very good. Earvin was six five or six six. He was average. Then I saw his next game. I never saw anything like it. He had 36 points, 18 rebounds, 5 steals, and 16 assists. It was against Jackson Parkside. And they were supposed to be one of the best teams around.

"I went down [to the locker room] and said, 'Man, Earvin, that was something else. We got to call you something.' Dr. J was taken. And The Big E was, too. I said, 'How about Magic?' And he said, 'That's OK with me.' "

Dr. J is the nickname for Julius Erving of the Philadelphia 76ers. The Big E is Elvin Hayes of the Washington Bullets. Magic likes his nickname.

Above: The Vikings pose for a picture.

Left: Magic and his high school coach, George Fox

Magic and
his father

"I think it fits," he says. "It makes me sound kind of mysterious. I guess some of the plays I make on the court are kind of magical. I don't know how they happen. It is instinct, I guess."

Magic was born in Lansing on August 14, 1959. He is one of 10 children. His father's name is Earvin, Sr. His mother's name is Christine.

Magic is not the only athlete in the family. A younger sister, Evelyn, goes to the University of South Carolina. She is on a basketball scholarship. She has a nickname, too. It is "The Sweet E." Magic says: "She's a pretty tough player."

Earvin, Sr. works very hard. His regular job is with the Fisher auto-body plant in Lansing. But over the years he has had to take second jobs. He has to care for his large family. He drove a garbage truck at one time. He also worked at a gas station. He believes that hard work pays off.

Magic admires his father.

"He always hoped we would do something in life," Magic says. "He didn't want me to ever work at the auto-body plant. My dad was important to me. He still is."

When Magic was a little boy, he and his dad used to watch NBA games on TV. Earvin, Sr. played basketball when he was a boy living in Mississippi. He knew the game well. He would explain it to young Earvin.

Magic and Reggie Chostine were co-captains during Magic's junior year. Chostine graduated in 1976 and was killed in an auto accident. The following season, the Vikings dedicated their games to him and won the state championship.

Magic began playing basketball on playgrounds. By the time he was in junior high, he was one of the best young players around. He always played against older guys. Some of them later played in the NBA. One was George Gervin, the NBA scoring champ. He plays for the San Antonio Spurs. They are good friends today.

By eighth grade, Magic stood six foot three. A year later, he was an inch taller.

Even on the playgrounds, winning was very important.

"When somebody would pick me to play on his team," says Magic, "I would ask who else he had. If he had a couple of guys who were great scorers but who could not play good defense or pass well,

I would say, 'No.' I would wait until I could play on a team that had a good rebounder and a good defensive player. Then we would have a good mix. We would have a good team. And we would win.''

Everett High had an average team. That was before Magic came. It had an 11-12 record. Magic changed all that.

"We knew we had a good player coming in," says George Fox. He was Magic's coach in high school.

Magic was better than good. During his first season, Everett had a record of 22-2. The next year it was 24-2. During Magic's senior season, Everett won the state championship. They finished the season with a 27-1 record.

Magic and Reggie Chostine worked hard to win.

Magic still slaps palms when a good shot is made.

Fox remembers Magic as an unselfish player.

"He was a senior," says Fox. "He was averaging 44 or 45 points the first four games. But we were not playing good team basketball. I said to him, 'Earvin, if you want to win the state, I think you better average about 23 points.' He said, 'I got you, coach.'

"That was all I had to say. I think he averaged 23.8 points the rest of the season. It was almost like he had it programmed."

Magic was wanted by many universities and colleges. They came from all over the country. This was during his senior year in high school. First he narrowed the list to UCLA, Maryland, North Carolina, Purdue, Indiana, Michigan and Michigan State.

Then he got down to the two Michigan schools. Both schools wanted him very badly. Magic was swayed by his father. His father wanted him to stay close to home. So Magic chose the state university across town in East Lansing.

Magic did for Michigan State what he had done for Everett High School.

Magic made Michigan State one of the best college basketball teams.

Before Magic, Michigan State had not been a major basketball power for years. In its last two seasons, its records were 14-13 and 10-17. With Magic, Michigan became one of the best teams. As a freshman, Magic led the Spartans to a 25-5 record. They lost to Kentucky, 52-49, in the Mideast Regional NCAA tournament. Kentucky went on to win the national title that season.

The next season, Magic and his teammates put it all together. They beat Indiana State for the NCAA title. Magic was the hero. He won the Most Valuable Player Award. After the game, he walked off the court. He had the basketball net hanging around his neck.

One of his biggest fans was Michigan State coach Jud Heathcote. At the time, he said Magic was the best basketball player in the world—pros included.

Heathcote remembers Magic. Magic played best when the pressure was greatest.

"Even though he never shot 50 percent for us," Heathcote said, "I'll bet he shot about 65 percent when a basket was needed. When he has to score or wants to score, he has a way of willing the ball into the basket."

Magic was faced with a hard choice after Michigan State won the NCAA championship in 1979. Should he stay in school for two more years and graduate? Or should he quit school and enter the NBA? In the NBA he could make a lot of money.

Magic wasn't always perfect.

Magic chose the NBA. He was the league's No. 1 draft choice in the college draft in June, 1979. The Los Angeles Lakers picked him. The Lakers signed him to a multi-year contract. It is thought to be $500,000 a year.

"It was a very difficult decision," says Magic. "All my friends wanted me to stay. But it was time to go. I had to think of my future in basketball. I could always go back to school during the summer. I could get enough credits to earn my degree."

Magic's major at Michigan State is communications. He played his rookie season with the Lakers. Then he returned to East Lansing. He continued his schooling.

Early in the season with the Lakers, Magic sprained a knee.

Before deciding, Magic talked to his father. Earvin, Sr. told him to do what Magic thought was best.

"When it came time to decide about the pros, I could not say that I wanted him to stay or go," remembers Magic's dad. "It seemed like he couldn't do anything more at Michigan State. They won the Big Ten Conference. They won the NCAA. After that, there didn't seem like there was anything left for him to do there."

Many people did not believe Magic would be a great player in the NBA. They said he did not shoot well. They said he did not jump well. They also said he would not have the same zest that he did in college. People said the NBA season was too long.

Magic plays any position the coach wants him to play.

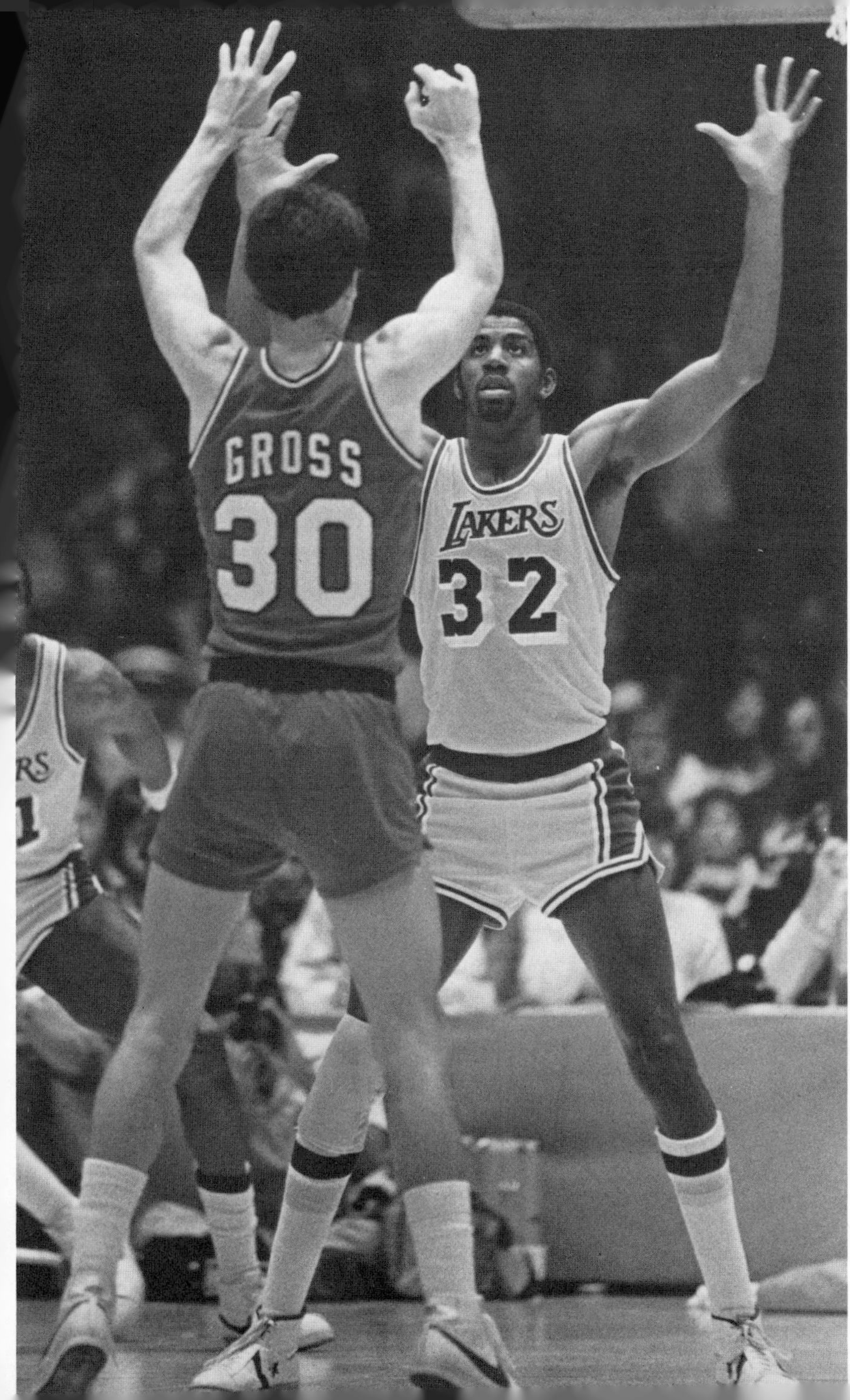
GROSS
30
LAKERS
32

Teams play as many as 100 games during the NBA season. In college, teams play 30 or so games.

Magic did not listen to the gripes. He went to his first training camp with the Lakers. Magic played as eagerly as in college. His new teammates liked the rookie's joy.

"I only play one way," Magic said at the time. "And that's all out. But I also play to have fun. This is a good team. We're going to have a lot of fun this season. We're going to be exciting. And the fans are going to enjoy us."

The Lakers were a good team. But people thought they were dull. Magic started at guard. The Lakers became a better team. They became exciting.

"Magic is not a rookie," said teammate Jamaal Wilkes. "He plays like he has been in the league forever."

"I think Magic has led us," said Kareem Abdul-Jabbar, another Laker teammate. "He gets smarter all the time. He's just like me. I was never really a rookie and neither was Magic."

Magic inspires his teammates. When a player makes a good play, he slaps his palm and cheers him on. Magic has fun playing basketball in the NBA. So do all of his teammates.

It did not take Magic long to adjust. The pro game is faster. It requires more strength than the college game. But he did have problems. He had injuries for the first time in his life.

Early in the season, he sprained a knee. Later, he suffered a groin injury. Once he was poked in the eye. Another time, he got cut on the head.

"I might be a little brittle," he said during the season. "But that's a result of the way I play. I play hard. And I don't mind taking the charges [charging fouls]. I never used to get hurt. Lately I've been getting hurt a lot."

Magic overcame his injuries. He led the Lakers to the league championship. It was their first since the 1971-72 season. He played in 77 of the Lakers' 82 regular-season games. He averaged 18 points. He shot 53.5 percent from the field. He was the NBA's best rebounding guard. He also finished the season ranked fifth in the league in steals. He ranked seventh in assists.

Magic prefers playing guard.

Magic started the season as the Lakers' point guard—the playmaker. But he also played forward at times. Bill Russell is a network broadcaster who was the all-star center of the Boston Celtics from 1956 to 1969. Russell said Magic could be the best power forward in the league.

Magic says he prefers playing guard. But he will play any position the coach wants him to.

"I don't care where I play so long as I play," he says. "That's what counts."

And Magic made it count during the championship finals against the Philadelphia 76ers. He was named the most valuable player.

In the sixth and final game of the best-of-seven series, Magic started at center. It was the first time since high school that he played center. He did so because the Lakers' starting center, Abdul-Jabbar, couldn't play. Abdul-Jabbar had sprained an ankle during the fifth game.

Laker coach Paul Westhead was expected to start forward Jim Chones at center. But Westhead surprised everybody, including Magic. He announced Magic would play center.

Magic was again at his best. In fact he played the best game of his life.

He started the game at center. But he played all five positions during the game. He was everywhere. And to the 76ers, he indeed was magic. He finished the game with 42 points and 15 rebounds. He also had seven assists, three steals,

and one blocked shot. They were the most points he had scored in one game since high school.

Abdul-Jabbar was injured. So the 76ers were expected to win the sixth game. A seventh game was to be played in Los Angeles two days later. The Lakers did not think a seventh game would be needed. It wasn't. The Lakers won.

"I'm a winner," Magic said. The Lakers were in the locker room after the game. They were very happy. "I think like a winner. I never go into a game thinking I can't win."

"Magic is truly Houdini," said coach Westhead. "He is a Magic Man. I knew if anybody could pull this out for us, he could do it.

"Everybody thinks of Magic as a fancy type of player. The kind of guy who makes the behind-

the-back pass or the dazzling play. But in reality, he is our blue-collar worker. He goes out there and works hard and bangs on the boards [for rebounds]. He never gives up until the game is over. He's one of a kind."

"We knew what we could do," said Chones. "We're an awesome team. We've known that all along. There wasn't any pressure on us. There never has been. We're the best."

One reason was Magic.

"Magic Johnson is the greatest young player of all time," continued Chones. "Out there on the court, he's telling you what you can do in life. He's saying that if you're enthusiastic and you try hard you can accomplish anything you want."

Magic also impressed the defeated 76ers.

"I knew he was good," said guard Doug Collins. "But I didn't know he was this good."

Julius Erving, the 76ers superstar forward, said: "He's the best rookie I've ever seen."

Abdul-Jabbar was proud of the rookie. "Words can't really describe him," he said. "He did everything: defense, offense, passing, shooting, rebounding, stealing the ball. There is nothing you can say he did not do."

Magic reached two of his goals in one pro season. First, he became one of the best players in the sport. Second, almost alone, he turned the Lakers into an exciting team. By the end of the year, the Lakers were the talk of Los Angeles. They were playing before full houses.

After the season, a reporter asked Magic what he would do for an encore.

"We're going to win it next year," he said. "And then we're going to win it again and again and again."

There is nothing in the world that Magic Johnson would rather do than win.

CHRONOLOGY

'59 —Earvin Johnson, Jr. is born in Lansing, Michigan on August 14.

'72 —As an eighth grader, Earvin, Jr. is a basketball star on the playgrounds.

'74 —Earvin, Jr. enters Everett High School in Lansing.

—Sportswriter Fred Stabley, Jr. gives Earvin the nickname, "Magic."

'77 —Everett High wins the Michigan state basketball championship.

—Magic decides to attend Michigan State University.

'78 —Led by Magic, who is a freshman, Michigan State finishes the season 25-5. It loses to Kentucky in the Mideast finals of the NCAA tournament.

'79 —Again led by Magic, Michigan State this time wins the NCAA tournament, beating Indiana State in the tournament. Magic is named the tournament's most valuable player.

—Magic decides to turn pro and is drafted by the Los Angeles Lakers as the No. 1 pick in the entire college draft.

'80 —Magic leads the Lakers to the NBA championship. He scores 42 points in the sixth and final game. He is named the playoffs' most valuable player.

ABOUT THE AUTHOR

Richard Levin is a sportswriter for the *Los Angeles Herald Examiner*. He has covered the Los Angeles Lakers the last seven years. He has been published in numerous sports magazines and co-authored a book, *Winning Basketball*, with Gail Goodrich.